EASY MASHED POTATOES COOKBOOK

50 SIMPLE AND DELICIOUS MASHED POTATO RECIPES

By
BookSumo Press
Copyright © by Saxonberg Associates

Published by
BookSumo Press, a DBA of Saxonberg Associates
http://www.booksumo.com/

ABOUT THE AUTHOR.

BookSumo Press is a publisher of unique, easy, and healthy cookbooks.

Our cookbooks span all topics and all subjects. If you want a deep dive into the possibilities of cooking with any type of ingredient. Then BookSumo Press is your go to place for robust yet simple and delicious cookbooks and recipes. Whether you are looking for great tasting pressure cooker recipes or authentic ethic and cultural food. BookSumo Press has a delicious and easy cookbook for you.

With simple ingredients, and even simpler step-by-step instructions BookSumo cookbooks get everyone in the kitchen chefing delicious meals.

BookSumo is an independent publisher of books operating in the beautiful Garden State (NJ) and our team of chefs and kitchen experts are here to teach, eat, and be merry!

INTRODUCTION

Welcome to *The Effortless Chef Series*! Thank you for taking the time to purchase this cookbook.

Come take a journey into the delights of easy cooking. The point of this cookbook and all BookSumo Press cookbooks is to exemplify the effortless nature of cooking simply.

In this book we focus on Mashed Potatoes. You will find that even though the recipes are simple, the taste of the dishes are quite amazing.

So will you take an adventure in simple cooking? If the answer is yes please consult the table of contents to find the dishes you are most interested in.

Once you are ready, jump right in and start cooking.

— BookSumo Press

TABLE OF CONTENTS

ANY ISSUES? CONTACT US

If you find that something important to you is missing from this book please contact us at info@booksumo.com.

We will take your concerns into consideration when the 2nd edition of this book is published. And we will keep you updated!

— BookSumo Press

LEGAL NOTES

COMMON ABBREVIATIONS

cup(s)	C.
tablespoon	tbsp
teaspoon	tsp
ounce	oz.
pound	lb

*All units used are standard American measurements

CHAPTER 1: EASY MASHED POTATOES RECIPES

CROCK POT STYLE MASH

Ingredients

- 5 lbs red potatoes, cut into chunks
- 1 tbsp minced garlic, or to taste
- 3 cubes chicken bouillon
- 1 (8 oz.) container sour cream
- 1 (8 oz.) package cream cheese, softened
- 1/2 C. butter
- salt and pepper to taste

Directions

- Get your potatoes boiling in water, bouillon, salt, and garlic for 17 mins.
- Then remove all the liquids to a separate bowl.
- Get a 2nd bowl and mash your potatoes in it. Then add the cream cheese and sour cream.
- Continue mashing everything but add some of the reserved liquids to keep the potatoes smooth.

- Now place everything into the crock of a slow cooker and let the potatoes cook for 3 hrs with a low level of heat.
- Add some pepper, salt, and the butter.
- Enjoy.

Amount per serving (8 total)

Timing Information:

Preparation	15 m
Cooking	3 h 15 m
Total Time	3 h 30 m

Nutritional Information:

Calories	470 kcal
Fat	27.7 g
Carbohydrates	47.9g
Protein	8.8 g
Cholesterol	74 mg
Sodium	703 mg

* Percent Daily Values are based on a 2,000 calorie diet.

Party-Time Romano and Garlic Mashed Potatoes

Ingredients

- 50 lbs unpeeled red potatoes, quartered
- 8 lbs butter, room temperature
- 3 lbs Romano cheese, grated
- 3 C. chopped garlic
- 1/2 C. salt
- 1/2 C. dried oregano

Directions

- Boil your potatoes in water and salt for 50 mins then remove all the liquids and add the potatoes to a bowl.
- Mash the potatoes with the oregano, butter, salt, garlic, and cheese.
- Once the mix is smooth serve it warm.
- Enjoy.

Amount per serving (100 total)

Timing Information:

Preparation	15 m
Cooking	45 m
Total Time	1 h

Nutritional Information:

Calories	498 kcal
Fat	33.4 g
Carbohydrates	43.2g
Protein	8.8 g
Cholesterol	92 mg
Sodium	940 mg

* Percent Daily Values are based on a 2,000 calorie diet.

CREAMY RANCH MASHED POTATOES

Ingredients

- 8 large potatoes, peeled and cubed
- 4 oz. cream cheese
- 1/3 C. butter
- 8 oz. sour cream
- 1/2 (1 oz.) package dry Ranch-style dressing mix

Directions

- Set your oven to 350 degrees before doing anything else.
- Begin to boil your potatoes in water for 12 mins then remove the liquids and add in the dressing mix, cream cheese, sour cream, and butter.
- Mash everything together then layer the potatoes into a casserole dish.
- Cook the contents in the oven for 35 mins.
- Enjoy.

Amount per serving (10 total)

Timing Information:

Preparation	30 m
Cooking	30 m
Total Time	1 h

Nutritional Information:

Calories	373 kcal
Fat	15.1 g
Carbohydrates	53.5g
Protein	7.6 g
Cholesterol	39 mg
Sodium	205 mg

* Percent Daily Values are based on a 2,000 calorie diet.

MILKY YUKON MASHED POTATOES

Ingredients

- 5 lbs Yukon Gold potatoes, cubed
- 2 (3 oz.) packages cream cheese
- 8 oz. sour cream
- 1/2 C. milk
- 2 tsps onion salt
- ground black pepper to taste

Directions

- Set your oven to 325 degrees before doing anything else.
- Get your potatoes boiling in water and salt for 20 mins then remove all the liquids and mash the potatoes in bowl.
- Once the potatoes are smooth combine in the pepper, cream cheese, onion salt, milk, and sour cream.
- Mash everything again then place the mix into a baking dish.
- Cook the potatoes in the oven for 55 mins with a covering of foil on the dish.
- Enjoy.

Amount per serving (12 total)

Timing Information:

Preparation	15 m
Cooking	1 h 5 m
Total Time	1 h 20 m

Nutritional Information:

Calories	245 kcal
Fat	9.3 g
Carbohydrates	35.8g
Protein	5.9 g
Cholesterol	25 mg
Sodium	370 mg

* Percent Daily Values are based on a 2,000 calorie diet.

OVEN ROASTED MASHED POTATOES

Ingredients

- 5 lbs Yukon Gold potatoes, peeled and cubed
- 1/2 C. butter
- 1/4 C. milk
- 1 (8 oz.) package cream cheese, softened
- 1 onion, grated
- 1 egg
- salt and pepper to taste

Directions

- Set your oven to 350 degrees before doing anything else.
- Boil your potatoes in water and salt for 20 mins then remove the liquids and mash the potatoes in a bowl.
- Add in the milk and butter and get a hand mixer.
- Begin to mix the potatoes then add in the onions and cream cheese.

- Get a 2nd bowl and whisk your eggs with a small amount of the potatoes.
- Once the egg mix is smooth add it to the potatoes and combine everything. Then add some pepper and salt.
- Lay everything into a baking dish and cook the potatoes in the oven for 60 mins.
- Enjoy.

Amount per serving (12 total)

Timing Information:

Preparation	20 m
Cooking	1 h 15 m
Total Time	1 h 35 m

Nutritional Information:

Calories	295 kcal
Fat	14.9 g
Carbohydrates	35.6g
Protein	6.2 g
Cholesterol	57 mg
Sodium	129 mg

* Percent Daily Values are based on a 2,000 calorie diet.

4 Ingredient Mashed Potatoes

Ingredients

- 2 lbs baking potatoes, peeled and quartered
- 2 tbsps butter
- 1 C. milk
- salt and pepper to taste

Directions

- Get your potatoes boiling in water and salt for 20 mins then remove all the liquids.
- Begin to heat and stir your milk and butter until the mix is smooth then add the milk mix to the potatoes and mash everything together.
- The potatoes should be smooth then add in some pepper and salt liberally and stir the spices into the potatoes.
- Enjoy.

Amount per serving (4 total)

Timing Information:

Preparation	15 m
Cooking	20 m
Total Time	35 m

Nutritional Information:

Calories	257 kcal
Fat	7.2 g
Carbohydrates	43.7g
Protein	5.6 g
Cholesterol	20 mg
Sodium	76 mg

* Percent Daily Values are based on a 2,000 calorie diet.

CANADIAN STYLE MASHED POTATOES

Ingredients

- 4 large sweet potatoes
- 1/2 C. softened butter
- 1 C. heavy cream
- 2 tbsps vanilla extract
- 1/2 C. packed light brown sugar
- 1 tsp salt
- 1/2 C. maple syrup
- 1 C. chopped pecans
- 2 eggs, beaten
- 2 tbsps maple syrup
- 1/4 C. chopped pecans

Directions

- Cover a cookie sheet with foil then set your oven to 375 degrees before doing anything else.

- Cook your sweet potatoes on the sheet, in the oven, for 55 mins. Then remove the skins on the potatoes when they are cool.
- Now coat a baking dish with butter and set the oven to 350 degrees before continuing.
- Place the sweet potatoes in a bowl and begin to mash them.
- Add in: the eggs, butter, 1 C. of pecans, cream, 1/2 C. syrup, vanilla, salt, and brown sugar.
- Continue to mash the potatoes until everything is combined nicely.
- Layer the mix into the baking dish and top the potatoes with the rest of the pecans and 2 tbsps of syrup.
- Cook the potatoes in the oven for 33 mins.
- Enjoy.

Amount per serving (12 total)

Timing Information:

Preparation	30 m
Cooking	1 h 15 m
Total Time	2 h 15 m

Nutritional Information:

Calories	448 kcal
Fat	24.9 g
Carbohydrates	53.1g
Protein	5.1 g
Cholesterol	79 mg
Sodium	355 mg

* Percent Daily Values are based on a 2,000 calorie diet.

New York Deli Mashed Potato Salad

Ingredients

- 5 red potatoes
- 5 Yukon Gold potatoes
- 2 tbsps butter
- salt and pepper to taste
- 1/2 C. mayonnaise
- 1/2 C. prepared mustard
- 1/2 C. sour cream
- 1 stalk celery, finely chopped
- 1 red onion, finely diced
- 2 small sweet pickles, finely chopped
- 1 green bell pepper, chopped

Directions

- Cut your potatoes into cubes then get them boiling in water and salt until they are soft.
- Remove the liquids then mash the potatoes in a bowl.

- Add in some pepper, salt, and the butter. Then continue to mash everything until it is all smooth.
- Now add in the sour cream, mustard, and mayo.
- Keep mashing the potatoes to evenly distribute the mayo and mustard then add in the green pepper, celery, pickles, and onions.
- Stir the new ingredients into the potatoes and then serve.
- Enjoy.

Amount per serving (6 total)

Timing Information:

Preparation	10 m
Cooking	20 m
Total Time	30 m

Nutritional Information:

Calories	457 kcal
Fat	23.6 g
Carbohydrates	56.8g
Protein	7.3 g
Cholesterol	26 mg
Sodium	420 mg

* Percent Daily Values are based on a 2,000 calorie diet.

Goat Cheese and Chives Mashed Potatoes

Ingredients

- 3 lbs Yukon Gold potatoes, cubed
- 1/2 C. butter
- 8 oz. goat cheese
- 3 tbsps chopped fresh dill
- 3 tbsps chopped fresh chives
- 1/2 C. milk

Directions

- Get your potatoes boiling in water and salt for 15 mins then remove the liquids and begin to mash the potatoes.
- Now add in the milk and butter and keep mashing until the potatoes are creamy.
- Now add the chives, goat cheese and dill.
- Stir the spices and cheese into the potatoes nicely then serve.
- Enjoy.

Amount per serving (8 total)

Timing Information:

Preparation	15 m
Cooking	10 m
Total Time	25 m

Nutritional Information:

Calories	348 kcal
Fat	20.5 g
Carbohydrates	32.2g
Protein	10.4 g
Cholesterol	54 mg
Sodium	245 mg

* Percent Daily Values are based on a 2,000 calorie diet.

SIMPLE SOUR CREAM MASHED POTATOES

Ingredients

- 3 Yukon Gold potatoes, peeled and chopped
- 1/3 C. milk
- 1/4 C. sour cream
- salt and ground black pepper to taste
- 1 tsp cayenne

Directions

- Get your potatoes boiling in water and salt for 25 mins then remove all the liquids.
- Place the potatoes in a bowl and begin to mash them.
- Now add some pepper, milk, some salt, and the sour cream.
- Mash everything until it is smooth then stir in the cayenne and serve the potatoes.
- Enjoy.

Amount per serving (2 total)

Timing Information:

Preparation	10 m
Cooking	20 m
Total Time	30 m

Nutritional Information:

Calories	226 kcal
Fat	7 g
Carbohydrates	36g
Protein	6 g
Cholesterol	16 mg
Sodium	237 mg

* Percent Daily Values are based on a 2,000 calorie diet.

MEDITERRANEAN MASHED POTATOES

Ingredients

- 3/4 lb turkey bacon, cut into 1 inch pieces
- 1 C. crumbled feta cheese
- 3 tbsps sour cream
- 1/8 tbsp dried oregano
- 1/8 tsp ground black pepper
- 3 (4 oz.) skinless, boneless chicken breast halves
- 1 C. all-purpose flour
- 2 eggs, beaten
- 1 C. dry bread crumbs
- 4 potatoes, peeled and cubed
- 1 sweet onion, chopped
- 2 tbsps butter
- 3 tbsps sour cream

Directions

- Set your oven to 350 degrees before doing anything else.
- Begin to fry your bacon until it is fully done then remove the pieces of bacon from the pan.
- Get a bowl, combine: bacon, black pepper, feta, oregano, and 3 tbsps of sour cream.

- Lay out your chicken breast and slice a small pocket into them with a sharp knife.
- Fill the breast with the feta mix.
- Get a bowl for your flour.
- Get a 2nd bowl for the eggs.
- Get a 3rd bowl for the bread crumbs.
- Coat your pieces of chicken with flour then the eggs and finally the bread crumbs.
- Fry the chicken for 4 mins each in the bacon drippings then place the meat into a casserole dish.
- Cook the chicken in the oven for 27 mins.
- At the same time get your potatoes boiling in water and salt for 22 mins with a lid on the pot. Then remove all the liquids.
- As the potatoes are cooking stir fry your onions for 12 mins in the bacon drippings then mash the potatoes with 3 tbsps of sour cream, butter, and onions.
- Serve the chicken with a side of potatoes.
- Enjoy.

Amount per serving (3 total)

Timing Information:

Preparation	30 m
Cooking	35 m
Total Time	1 h 5 m

Nutritional Information:

Calories	1498 kcal
Fat	84.2 g
Carbohydrates	1118.9g
Protein	64.7 g
Cholesterol	1343 mg
Sodium	11961 mg

* Percent Daily Values are based on a 2,000 calorie diet.

Cheddar and Mashed Potatoes Roasted

Ingredients

- 2 large baking potatoes
- 1/2 lb lean bacon
- 3/4 C. shredded mild Cheddar cheese
- 1/2 C. sour cream
- 1/4 C. milk
- 2 tbsps unsalted butter, melted
- 1 tsp dried chives
- 1/2 tsp salt
- 1/2 tsp ground black pepper
- 1/2 tsp garlic powder
- 3/4 C. shredded mild Cheddar cheese

Directions

- Coat a baking dish with oil then set your oven to 400 degrees before doing anything else.

- Pierce your potatoes with a fork then cook them in the oven for 60 mins.
- Now let the potatoes sit until they are no longer hot.
- At the same time begin to fry your bacon for 12 mins then break the bacon into pieces and place them on some paper towels.
- Cut the tops from the potatoes and remove the insides or.
- Now mash the potatoes without any skin, in a bowl, then add in: the garlic powder, 3/4 C. cheddar, black pepper, sour cream, salt, milk, chives, and butter.
- Place everything into the baking dish and top it all with another 3/4 C. of cheddar and the bacon.
- Cook everything in the oven for 12 mins.
- Enjoy.

Amount per serving (4 total)

Timing Information:

Preparation	15 m
Cooking	1 h 10 m
Total Time	1 h 30 m

Nutritional Information:

Calories	535 kcal
Fat	34 g
Carbohydrates	35.4g
Protein	22.7 g
Cholesterol	94 mg
Sodium	1015 mg

* Percent Daily Values are based on a 2,000 calorie diet.

RUSTIC STYLE MASHED POTATOES

Ingredients

- 5 lbs potatoes, peeled and cubed
- 6 oz. cream cheese, softened
- 1 C. sour cream
- 1 tbsp freeze-dried chives
- salt and pepper to taste
- 1/8 tsp paprika
- 1/4 C. butter

Directions

- Get your potatoes boiling in water and salt for 25 mins then remove the liquids and mash the spuds with: some pepper, some salt, cream cheese, chives, and sour cream.
- Once the mix is smooth place the potatoes in the fridge until they are chilled.
- Now coat a baking dish with nonstick spray and lay your potatoes in it.

- Cook the potatoes in the oven for 35 mins.
- Enjoy.

Amount per serving (12 total)

Timing Information:

Preparation	30 m
Cooking	30 m
Total Time	1 h

Nutritional Information:

Calories	271 kcal
Fat	13 g
Carbohydrates	35.3g
Protein	4.6 g
Cholesterol	34 mg
Sodium	490 mg

* Percent Daily Values are based on a 2,000 calorie diet.

BACKROAD BACON MASHED POTATOES

Ingredients

- 6 Yukon Gold potatoes, peeled and quartered
- 5 slices turkey bacon
- 1 tbsp vegetable oil
- 6 medium mushrooms, sliced
- 1 medium onion, sliced
- 2 tbsps butter
- 2 tbsps ranch dressing

Directions

- Get your potatoes boiling in water and salt for 25 mins.
- At the same time fry your bacon until it is fully done and crisp then place them on some paper towels to drain.
- Now begin to stir fry your onions and mushrooms in the bacon fat with some veggie oil until the onions are see-through.
- Remove the liquid from the potatoes then begin to mash them in bowl with the dressing and butter.

- Once the potatoes are smooth add in the bacon after breaking it into pieces.
- Stir the bacon into the potatoes then add in the onions and mushrooms.
- Enjoy.

Amount per serving (6 total)

Timing Information:

Preparation	20 m
Cooking	30 m
Total Time	50 m

Nutritional Information:

Calories	293 kcal
Fat	19.4 g
Carbohydrates	24.6g
Protein	6.1 g
Cholesterol	27 mg
Sodium	278 mg

* Percent Daily Values are based on a 2,000 calorie diet.

Pears and Sweet Mashed Potatoes

Ingredients

- 3 lbs sweet potatoes, cleaned, dried
- 1/3 C. butter
- 1 (15.25 oz.) can pears in syrup
- 2 tbsps chopped fresh sage
- Salt and black pepper

Directions

- Set your oven to 425 degrees before doing anything else.
- Pierce your sweet potatoes with a toothpick and cook them in the oven for 55 mins.
- At the same time heat and stir your butter for 11 mins then shut the heat.
- Cut your potatoes into halves and remove the insides into the pot with butter.
- Mash the potatoes with the sage and pears in the butter and get everything hot.

- Add some pepper and salt.
- Enjoy.

Amount per serving (8 total)

Timing Information:

Preparation	20 m
Cooking	40 m
Total Time	1 h

Nutritional Information:

Calories	257 kcal
Fat	7.8 g
Carbohydrates	44.6g
Protein	2.8 g
Cholesterol	20 mg
Sodium	201 mg

* Percent Daily Values are based on a 2,000 calorie diet.

ARTISAN MASHED POTATOES

Ingredients

- 2 russet potatoes, peeled and cut into chunks
- 1 large celery root, peeled and cut into chunks
- 1/4 C. butter
- 1 pinch freshly grated nutmeg, or to taste
- salt and freshly ground black pepper to taste
- 1/4 C. heavy whipping cream

Directions

- Get your celery and potatoes boiling in water and salt for 25 mins then remove the liquids and combine everything together.
- Get a bowl and begin to mash the potatoes with some black pepper, butter, salt, and nutmeg.
- Then add in the cream and mash everything again.
- Enjoy.

Amount per serving (4 total)

Timing Information:

Preparation	15 m
Cooking	20 m
Total Time	35 m

Nutritional Information:

Calories	320 kcal
Fat	17.8 g
Carbohydrates	37.6g
Protein	5.6 g
Cholesterol	51 mg
Sodium	333 mg

* Percent Daily Values are based on a 2,000 calorie diet.

TURKEY TARRAGON MASHED POTATOES

Ingredients

- 1 (12 oz.) package turkey bacon
- 5 lbs russet potatoes, peeled and diced
- 1 (32 oz.) carton chicken Stock
- 1/4 C. low-fat sour cream
- 1/4 C. low-sodium dry ranch dressing mix
- 3/4 C. shredded nonfat Cheddar cheese
- 1 tbsp chopped fresh chives
- 2 tbsps tarragon

Directions

- Fry your bacon until fully done then break it into pieces as you remove it from the pan.
- Get your potatoes boiling in broth for 17 mins then shut the heat.
- Add in the ranch and sour cream.
- Mash the potatoes until they are smooth and creamy with a mixer for 5 mins then add in the chives, tarragon, cheddar, and bacon.

- Stir everything again.
- Enjoy.

Amount per serving (10 total)

Timing Information:

Preparation	15 m
Cooking	15 m
Total Time	30 m

Nutritional Information:

Calories	240 kcal
Fat	3.2 g
Carbohydrates	42.9g
Protein	11 g
Cholesterol	13 mg
Sodium	372 mg

* Percent Daily Values are based on a 2,000 calorie diet.

Mashed Potatoes for Autumn

Ingredients

- 2 lbs russet potatoes, peeled and cut into cubes
- 1 lb sweet potatoes, peeled and cut into cubes
- 1 tbsp chicken bouillon granules
- 3/4 C. milk, warmed
- 1/4 C. butter
- 1 1/2 tbsps brown sugar
- 1 tsp salt
- 1/4 tsp ground white pepper
- 1/4 tsp allspice
- 1/8 tsp ground nutmeg

Directions

- Get both types of potatoes boiling in water with the bouillon.
- Once the potatoes are boiling, set the heat to medium and continue to cook them for 22 mins.
- Now remove all the liquids and mash the potatoes partially.

- Add in: the nutmeg, milk, allspice, butter, pepper, brown sugar, and salt.
- Begin to mash the potatoes again until everything is smooth.
- Enjoy.

Amount per serving (8 total)

Timing Information:

Preparation	20 m
Cooking	15 m
Total Time	35 m

Nutritional Information:

Calories	213 kcal
Fat	6.5 g
Carbohydrates	35.7g
Protein	4.3 g
Cholesterol	17 mg
Sodium	519 mg

* Percent Daily Values are based on a 2,000 calorie diet.

MASHED POTATOES INDIAN BREAD

Ingredients

- 1 C. mashed potatoes
- salt to taste
- 1/2 tsp cayenne pepper
- 1/2 tsp ground turmeric
- 1 tbsp fresh cilantro, finely chopped
- 3 tbsps vegetable oil
- 2 C. whole wheat flour
- 3/4 C. vegetable oil for frying
- 1 tbsp butter, melted

Directions

- Get a bowl, combine: 3 tbsps veggie oil, mashed potatoes, cilantro, salt, turmeric, cayenne, and salt.
- Now slowly add in the wheat flour then work the mix into a dough.
- Place the dough in bowl coated with oil and place a covering of plastic on the bowl.

- Let the dough sit for 12 mins.
- Now begin to heat a griddle coated with nonstick spray.
- Break your dough into balls then flatten the balls to a quarter of an inch.
- Fry the flattened dough in 1 tsp of oil for each side.
- Keep frying the bread until brown portions begin to show.
- Top each piece with some butter.
- Enjoy.

Amount per serving (4 total)

Timing Information:

Preparation	30 m
Cooking	15 m
Total Time	45 m

Nutritional Information:

Calories	400 kcal
Fat	18.6 g
Carbohydrates	53.1g
Protein	9.3 g
Cholesterol	9 mg
Sodium	183 mg

* Percent Daily Values are based on a 2,000 calorie diet.

MASHED POTATOES AND PESTO

Ingredients

- 4 medium potatoes, peeled and cubed
- 1 tbsp butter
- 1/4 C. milk, or as needed
- 1 tbsp basil pesto

Directions

- Get your potatoes boiling in water for 15 mins then remove all the liquids.
- Begin to the mash the potatoes partially then add in the milk and butter.
- Continue to mash the potatoes then add in the pesto and keep mashing everything until the pesto is evenly distributed and the potatoes are smooth.
- Enjoy.

Amount per serving (4 total)

Timing Information:

Preparation	5 m
Cooking	25 m
Total Time	30 m

Nutritional Information:

Calories	216 kcal
Fat	5.1 g
Carbohydrates	38.2g
Protein	5.5 g
Cholesterol	10 mg
Sodium	69 mg

* Percent Daily Values are based on a 2,000 calorie diet.

MASHED POTATO MEATLOAF

Ingredients

- 1 C. diced onion
- 1 C. instant mashed potatoes
- 1 C. diced green bell pepper
- 1/4 C. hot pepper sauce
- 1 egg
- 1 tsp salt
- 1 tsp ground black pepper
- 2 lbs ground beef
- 1 (.75 oz.) packet dry brown gravy mix

Directions

- Set your oven to 350 degrees before doing anything else.
- Get a bowl, combine: pepper, onion, salt, bell pepper, eggs, instant potatoes, and hot sauce.
- Stir the mix then add in the beef and combine everything evenly.
- Place the beef into a bread pan and top it with the gravy mix.

- Cook the meatloaf in the oven for 60 mins then let it sit for 15 mins before slicing it into pieces.
- Enjoy.

Amount per serving (6 total)

Timing Information:

Preparation	15 m
Cooking	1 h
Total Time	1 h 15 m

Nutritional Information:

Calories	396 kcal
Fat	23.8 g
Carbohydrates	16g
Protein	27.8 g
Cholesterol	122 mg
Sodium	979 mg

* Percent Daily Values are based on a 2,000 calorie diet.

SCALLIONS, MUSHROOMS, AND MASHED POTATOES

Ingredients

- 1 (4 oz.) package Flavored Mashed Potatoes Flakes
- 2 large Portobello mushrooms, cleaned
- Oil
- Salt and pepper
- 1/2 C. Cheddar cheese, shredded
- 2 tbsps bell pepper, diced and lightly sautéed
- 2 tbsps scallions, chopped

Directions

- Set your oven to 350 degrees before doing anything else.
- Coat your mushrooms with oil, pepper, and salt. Then place them on a cookie sheet covered with foil.
- Cook the mushrooms in the oven for 7 mins.
- At the same time prepare your flavored instant potatoes in line with the directions on the package.

- Add in the peppers and cheese to the potatoes.
- Now top your mushrooms with more salt and fill them with the potatoes.
- Garnish everything with the scallions.
- Enjoy.

Amount per serving (4 total)

Timing Information:

Preparation	15 m
Cooking	5 m
Total Time	20 m

Nutritional Information:

Calories	88 kcal
Fat	5.5 g
Carbohydrates	5.6g
Protein	4.1 g
Cholesterol	15 mg
Sodium	333 mg

* Percent Daily Values are based on a 2,000 calorie diet.

RUSTIC ROLLS

Ingredients

- 1/3 C. Original Mashed Potatoes Flakes, dry
- 1/4 C. warm water (110 degrees to 115 degrees F)
- 2 tbsps sugar
- 1 (.25 oz.) envelope active dry yeast*
- 2 3/4 C. all-purpose flour
- 1/2 tsp salt
- 3/4 C. warm milk, scalded and cooled to luke warm
- 2 tbsps butter
- 1 egg
- Melted butter for brushing

Directions

- Get a bowl, combine: sugar and warm water.
- Pour your yeast on top of the mix and let it stand for 15 mins.
- Get a 2nd bowl combine: salt and flour. Then add in the dry potatoes.

- Get a 3rd bowl, combine: eggs, yeast mix, butter, and milk.
- Gradually add in your flour mix until you form a dough.
- Put the dough in a 3rd bowl coated with oil and top the dough with melted butter.
- Place a kitchen towel over the bowl and let the dough sit until it has doubled in size.
- Now set your oven to 425 degrees before doing anything else.
- Knead the dough on a cutting board coated with flour and roll it out.
- Slice the dough with a biscuit cutter then place the biscuits onto a cookie sheet.
- Let the dough sit again for 50 mins.
- Now cook your rolls in the oven for 30 mins.
- Enjoy.

Amount per serving (18 total)

Timing Information:

Preparation	25 m
Cooking	25 m
Total Time	1 h 50 m

Nutritional Information:

Calories	102 kcal
Fat	2.6 g
Carbohydrates	16.6g
Protein	2.8 g
Cholesterol	15 mg
Sodium	86 mg

* Percent Daily Values are based on a 2,000 calorie diet.

Easy American Mashed Potatoes

Ingredients

- 1 (4 oz.) package Idahoan(R) Baby Reds Flavored Mashed Potatoes
- 1 (2.5 oz.) package bacon pieces
- 1/2 C. blue cheese crumbles

Directions

- Cook your potatoes in line with the directions on the package then add in the cheese and the bacon.
- Enjoy.

Amount per serving (4 total)

Timing Information:

Preparation	10 m
Cooking	30 m
Total Time	40 m

Nutritional Information:

Calories	151 kcal
Fat	9.5 g
Carbohydrates	5.6g
Protein	11.8 g
Cholesterol	26 mg
Sodium	901 mg

* Percent Daily Values are based on a 2,000 calorie diet.

BEANS AND MASHED POTATOES

Ingredients

- 1 (4 oz.) package Idahoan(R) Buttery Homestyle Flavored Mashed Potatoes, prepared
- 1 (10.75 oz.) can condensed cream of mushroom soup
- 3/4 C. milk
- 1/8 tsp ground black pepper
- 2 (15 oz.) cans green beans, drained*
- 1 1/3 C. French's(R) French Fried Onions, divided

Directions

- Set your oven to 350 degrees before doing anything else.
- Get a bowl, combine: green beans, soup, pepper, and milk.
- Stir the mix then add in 2/3 C. of fried onions.
- Spread everything into a baking dish and top the dish with some of the potatoes.
- For 4 mins toast everything under the broiler then add the rest of the fried onions.
- Enjoy.

Amount per serving (8 total)

Timing Information:

Preparation	10 m
Cooking	20 m
Total Time	30 m

Nutritional Information:

Calories	119 kcal
Fat	7.4 g
Carbohydrates	10.5g
Protein	2.1 g
Cholesterol	2 mg
Sodium	507 mg

* Percent Daily Values are based on a 2,000 calorie diet.

MASHED POTATOES AND GOUDA

Ingredients

- 1 (4 oz.) package Idahoan(R) Buttery Golden Selects Mashed Potatoes
- 1 (3 oz.) package bacon bits*
- 1/2 C. Gouda cheese, shredded

Directions

- Cook your potatoes in line with its associated directions then add in the cheese and bacon.
- Stir the bacon and cheese into the potatoes.
- Enjoy.

Amount per serving (4 total)

Timing Information:

Preparation	
Cooking	5 m
Total Time	5 m

Nutritional Information:

Calories	128 kcal
Fat	8.6 g
Carbohydrates	0.3g
Protein	12.7 g
Cholesterol	32 mg
Sodium	783 mg

* Percent Daily Values are based on a 2,000 calorie diet.

Maria's Potato Cannoli

Ingredients

- 2 C. shredded Parmesan cheese
- 1 (4 oz.) package Flavored Mashed Potatoes, prepared
- 2 tbsps green onion, washed and chopped fine
- 1 tbsp Italian parsley, chopped

Directions

- Spread your parmesan in the center of a hot skillet and fry the cheese for 2 mins.
- Flip the cheese and cook it for 2 more mins.
- Now use the handle of wooden as a guide for shaping your cheese into a hollow cylinder.
- Continue doing this until you have made twenty five hollow cylinders.
- Prepare your potatoes in line with their associated directions then then add in the parsley and onions. Stir the mix then place a cover over everything.

- Now fill a pastry bag with the potatoes and use the bag to fill the hollowed parmesan cylinders with the potatoes.
- Enjoy.

Amount per serving (25 total)

Timing Information:

Preparation	10 m
Cooking	20 m
Total Time	30 m

Nutritional Information:

Calories	27 kcal
Fat	1.8 g
Carbohydrates	0.3g
Protein	2.4 g
Cholesterol	5 mg
Sodium	109 mg

* Percent Daily Values are based on a 2,000 calorie diet.

MASHED POTATOES CAKES

Ingredients

- 1 1/2 C. grated raw potatoes
- 1 C. all-purpose flour
- 1/2 C. shredded Cheddar cheese
- 1 C. leftover mashed potatoes
- 1/4 tsp salt
- 1/4 tsp ground black pepper
- 1 egg
- 2 tbsps ranch dressing
- 1 tbsp milk
- 2 tbsps vegetable oil

Directions

- Get a bowl, combine: the flour and potatoes.
- Add in the cheese, some pepper, and salt.
- Stir the cheese into the potatoes.
- Get a 2nd bowl, combine: milk, egg, and ranch dressing.

- Once the mix is smooth combine both bowls and stir everything again.
- Now get your veggie oil hot for frying then fry tbsp sized dollops of the mix in the pan for 5 mins each side.
- Enjoy.

Amount per serving (6 total)

Timing Information:

Preparation	15 m
Cooking	10 m
Total Time	25 m

Nutritional Information:

Calories	261 kcal
Fat	12.8 g
Carbohydrates	29.2g
Protein	7.2 g
Cholesterol	43 mg
Sodium	335 mg

* Percent Daily Values are based on a 2,000 calorie diet.

ARMADILLO MASHED POTATOES

Ingredients

- 4 large potatoes, peeled and cubed
- 1 C. sour cream
- 1 (8 oz.) package cream cheese, softened
- 2 tbsps minced green onion
- salt and pepper to taste
- 1/4 C. slivered almonds
- 2 tbsps butter, melted
- 1/4 C. bread crumbs

Directions

- Coat a baking dish with butter then set your oven to 350 degrees before doing anything else.
- Get your potatoes boiling in water and salt.
- Once the potatoes are boiling set the heat to low, place a lid on the pot, and let the potatoes cook for 22 mins.

- Now remove all the liquids and place the potatoes in a bowl and mash them.
- Add in the pepper, sour cream, salt, cream cheese, and green onions to the potatoes and begin to continue mashing everything with a mixer or masher until smooth.
- Spread the potatoes into the baking dish and top everything with almonds.
- Top the almonds with butter and bread crumbs.
- Cook the contents in the oven for 35 mins.
- Enjoy.

Amount per serving (6 total)

Timing Information:

Preparation	20 m
Cooking	55 m
Total Time	1 h 15 m

Nutritional Information:

Calories	481 kcal
Fat	27.6 g
Carbohydrates	49.9g
Protein	10.6 g
Cholesterol	68 mg
Sodium	232 mg

* Percent Daily Values are based on a 2,000 calorie diet.

French Style Gratin with Mashed Potatoes

Ingredients

- Unsalted butter
- 2 1/2 C. chicken broth
- 4 large russet potatoes, peeled, diced
- 1 tsp salt
- 1/4 C. unsalted butter
- 4 cloves garlic, finely chopped
- 1/2 C. grated Parmesan cheese
- Salt and pepper to taste
- 1/2 C. panko bread crumbs

Directions

- Coat a baking dish with butter then set your oven to 375 degrees before doing anything else.
- Add your broth to a large pot and combine in 1 tsp of salt and your potatoes.

- Get everything boiling.
- Once the potatoes are boiling, place a lid on the pot, set the heat to low, and let everything cook for 15 mins.
- Remove the potatoes from the liquid to a bowl.
- Place the broth in a separate bowl as well.
- Clean the pot then add in 2 tbsps of butter and begin to stir fry your garlic in it for 4 mins.
- Add the potatoes into the pot and mash them with the butter and garlic.
- Add in 1 C. of broth and continue mashing.
- Now stir in the 1/4 C. of cheese and more 2 tbsp of butter.
- Add some pepper and salt if you like.
- Spread the potatoes into the baking dish and top it with the rest of the cheese and the bread crumbs.
- Cook everything in the oven for 25 mins.
- Enjoy.

Amount per serving (9 total)

Timing Information:

Preparation	10 m
Cooking	30 m
Total Time	40 m

Nutritional Information:

Calories	263 kcal
Fat	9.6 g
Carbohydrates	37.7g
Protein	7 g
Cholesterol	19 mg
Sodium	739 mg

* Percent Daily Values are based on a 2,000 calorie diet.

Italian Style Mashed Potatoes

Ingredients

- 2 lbs potatoes, scrubbed and chopped
- 2 tbsps butter
- 2 oz. cream cheese
- 1/3 C. sour cream
- 2 tsps dried basil
- 1/2 tsp garlic powder
- salt and ground black pepper to taste

Directions

- Get your potatoes boiling in water and salt, place a lid on the pot, set the heat to low, and let everything cook for 25 mins.
-
- Remove all the liquid and being to partially mash your potatoes.
- Add in: the garlic powder, butter, basil, cream cheese, and sour cream.

- Mash the potatoes until they are smooth then add in some pepper and salt.
- Enjoy.

Amount per serving (6 total)

Timing Information:

Preparation	10 m
Cooking	20 m
Total Time	30 m

Nutritional Information:

Calories	212 kcal
Fat	10 g
Carbohydrates	27.5g
Protein	4.3 g
Cholesterol	26 mg
Sodium	136 mg

* Percent Daily Values are based on a 2,000 calorie diet.

5 INGREDIENT MASHED POTATOES

Ingredients

- 4 large potatoes
- 1/4 C. butter
- 2 tsps ground nutmeg, or to taste
- 2 tsps salt, or to taste
- 1/2 C. sour cream

Directions

- Get your potatoes boiling in water and salt, place a lid on the pot, set the heat to low, and let the potatoes cook for 22 mins.
- Remove all the liquid and partially mash the potatoes.
- Add in your salt, nutmeg, and butter and fully mash everything then add in the sour cream and stir the cream into the potatoes.
- Enjoy.

Amount per serving (6 total)

Timing Information:

Preparation	10 m
Cooking	20 m
Total Time	30 m

Nutritional Information:

Calories	304 kcal
Fat	12.3 g
Carbohydrates	44.3g
Protein	5.7 g
Cholesterol	29 mg
Sodium	801 mg

* Percent Daily Values are based on a 2,000 calorie diet.

Tangy Mashed Potatoes

Ingredients

- 5 potatoes, peeled and quartered
- 2 tbsps butter, divided
- ground black pepper to taste
- 1/2 C. sour cream
- 1 tbsp prepared horseradish
- 2 tsps minced parsley

Directions

- Get your potatoes boiling in water and salt for 17 mins then remove all the liquids and add in some black pepper, and 1 tbsp of butter.
- Mash everything together then add the parsley, horseradish and sour cream.
- Mash everything together again then place it all in bowl for serving.
- Top the potatoes with 1 tbsp of butter.
- Enjoy.

Amount per serving (4 total)

Timing Information:

Preparation	5 m
Cooking	15 m
Total Time	20 m

Nutritional Information:

Calories	321 kcal
Fat	12.1 g
Carbohydrates	49.6g
Protein	5.1 g
Cholesterol	28 mg
Sodium	80 mg

* Percent Daily Values are based on a 2,000 calorie diet.

Asian Style Mashed Potatoes

Ingredients

- 5 potatoes, peeled and quartered
- 3 tbsps butter
- 1/4 C. of sriracha
- 1/8 C. milk

Directions

- Get your potatoes boiling in water and salt for 14 mins.
- Remove the liquid and begin to mash the potatoes in a bowl.
- Then add in the milk and butter and continue mashing until everything is smooth.
- Now add the sriracha and stir it in.
- Enjoy.

Amount per serving (5 total)

Timing Information:

Preparation	15 m
Cooking	10 m
Total Time	25 m

Nutritional Information:

Calories	228 kcal
Fat	7.2 g
Carbohydrates	37.5g
Protein	4.6 g
Cholesterol	19 mg
Sodium	64 mg

* Percent Daily Values are based on a 2,000 calorie diet.

Japanese Style Mashed Potatoes

Ingredients

- 1 medium head garlic
- 1 tsp olive oil
- 12 potatoes, skin removed, cut into quarters
- 1 C. butter, softened
- 4 tsps wasabi powder
- water as needed
- 1/2 C. milk
- salt and pepper to taste

Directions

- Set your oven to 400 degrees before doing anything else.
- Take off the skins of your garlic then coat the pieces with the olive oil.
- Place the garlic on a cookie sheet and toast everything in the oven for 50 mins.

- At the same time begin to boil your potatoes in water and salt for 22 mins.
- Remove the liquids and begin to mash the potatoes with the butter until smooth.
- Remove any remaining skin on your garlic and place the garlic into a bowl.
- Combine your wasabi and some water to make a paste then combine the garlic and wasabi paste together.
- Once everything is smooth add the wasabi mix to the potatoes and mash everything together.
- Now add in your milk and mash everything one more time.
- Top the potatoes with some pepper and salt.
- Enjoy.

Amount per serving (6 total)

Timing Information:

Preparation	15 m
Cooking	45 m
Total Time	1 h

Nutritional Information:

Calories	635 kcal
Fat	32.3 g
Carbohydrates	81.5g
Protein	8.2 g
Cholesterol	83 mg
Sodium	250 mg

* Percent Daily Values are based on a 2,000 calorie diet.

IRISH STYLE MASHED POTATOES

Ingredients

- 1 (4 oz.) package Idahoan(R) Buttery Homestyle Flavored Mashed Potatoes
- olive oil
- 1 (12 oz.) package chicken sausage*
- 1 head cabbage, core removed, cut into 4 pieces
- 1 tbsp chicken stock
- 1 tbsp balsamic vinegar
- Sea salt
- Ground pepper
- 2 tbsps stone ground mustard

Directions

- Grease a Dutch oven with oil then slice your sausages and begin to fry them until they are fully done.
- Remove the sausages from the pot then add in the cabbage and begin to fry it.

- Let the cabbage cook until it is somewhat soft then add in the stock, place a lid on the pot, and let the cabbage fully cook.
- Add in some balsamic when the cabbage is done and add in the sausage some pepper and some salt as well.
- Let the cabbage cook as you make your potatoes in line with their associated directions.
- Add the mustard to the potatoes and stir everything.
- Serve the potatoes with a side of cabbage topped with more balsamic.
- Enjoy.

Amount per serving (4 total)

Timing Information:

Preparation	15 m
Cooking	40 m
Total Time	55 m

Nutritional Information:

Calories	223 kcal
Fat	8.1 g
Carbohydrates	22.4g
Protein	16 g
Cholesterol	53 mg
Sodium	994 mg

* Percent Daily Values are based on a 2,000 calorie diet.

MASHED POTATOES RE-IMAGINED

Ingredients

- 3 large sweet potatoes, peeled and chopped
- 3 tbsps butter
- 2 tbsps chicken bouillon granules
- 1 tbsp ground black pepper
- 1 1/2 tsps white truffle oil
- 1 tsp garlic powder

Directions

- Get your potatoes boiling in water for 17 mins then remove the liquids and being to partially mash the potatoes.
- Add in the garlic powder, butter, truffle oil, bouillon, and black pepper and mash everything until it is smooth.
- Enjoy.

Amount per serving (6 total)

Timing Information:

Preparation	10 m
Cooking	15 m
Total Time	25 m

Nutritional Information:

Calories	266 kcal
Fat	7.4 g
Carbohydrates	47.1g
Protein	4.2 g
Cholesterol	16 mg
Sodium	541 mg

* Percent Daily Values are based on a 2,000 calorie diet.

Persian Style Mashed Potatoes

Ingredients

- 5 C. chicken stock
- 1 lb Yukon Gold potatoes
- 1 clove garlic, minced
- 1 tsp saffron threads, crushed
- 1/2 C. milk
- 2 tbsps olive oil
- salt and ground black pepper to taste

Directions

- Get your saffron, stock, garlic, and potatoes boiling.
- Place a lid on the pot, and lower the heat.
- Let the potatoes cook for 22 mins then remove all the liquids and save the stock for another recipe.
- Begin to partially mash the potatoes then add in some black pepper, milk, salt, and olive oil.
- Mash everything until it is smooth.
- Enjoy.

Amount per serving (4 total)

Timing Information:

Preparation	15 m
Cooking	20 m
Total Time	35 m

Nutritional Information:

Calories	180 kcal
Fat	8.2 g
Carbohydrates	23.5g
Protein	4.2 g
Cholesterol	3 mg
Sodium	877 mg

* Percent Daily Values are based on a 2,000 calorie diet.

GRANNY SMITH MASHED POTATOES

Ingredients

- 2 C. water, divided
- 1 tsp brown sugar
- 1 small lemon, halved and juiced, halves reserved
- 1 large granny smith apple, peeled and chopped
- 4 large baking potatoes, peeled and chopped
- 6 C. water
- 3 tbsps butter
- 3 tbsps heavy whipping cream
- 1 tsp salt
- 1 tbsp ground black pepper

Directions

- Get the following boiling: apple, 2 C. water, juiced lemon halves, brown sugar, and lemon juice.
- Let the mix boil for 14 mins then remove the lemon halves and throw them away.

- Drain the mix and keep the apples warm with a very low level of heat.
- Get your potatoes boiling in 6 C. of water for 22 mins then remove all the liquids again.
- Now being to mash your apples and potatoes together then add in the black pepper, butter, salt, and whipping cream.
- Mash everything until it is smooth.
- Enjoy.

Amount per serving (6 total)

Timing Information:

Preparation	15 m
Cooking	25 m
Total Time	40 m

Nutritional Information:

Calories	293 kcal
Fat	8.9 g
Carbohydrates	51g
Protein	5.6 g
Cholesterol	25 mg
Sodium	457 mg

* Percent Daily Values are based on a 2,000 calorie diet.

HASH BROWN SOUP

Ingredients

- 4 1/2 tbsps butter
- 1 1/2 C. frozen chopped onions
- 1 1/2 (14.5 oz.) cans chicken broth
- 1 (24 oz.) package frozen hash brown potatoes (such as Ore-Ida(R) Steam n' Mash(R)) Garlic Seasoned Potatoes)
- 3 tbsps all-purpose flour
- 1 1/2 tsps dried basil
- 3/4 tsp salt
- 3/4 tsp ground black pepper
- 3/4 tsp garlic salt
- 1 1/2 dashes hot sauce
- 1 (12 oz.) can evaporated milk

Directions

- Stir fry your onions in butter for 7 mins then add in: the broth, hot sauce, potatoes, garlic salt, flour, pepper, basil and salt.
- Get everything boiling, set the heat to low, and let the potatoes cook for 22 mins.
- Add in the evaporated milk and stir the mix evenly.
- Enjoy.

Amount per serving (6 total)

Timing Information:

Preparation	10 m
Cooking	25 m
Total Time	35 m

Nutritional Information:

Calories	284 kcal
Fat	14 g
Carbohydrates	33.4g
Protein	7.7 g
Cholesterol	42 mg
Sodium	1112 mg

* Percent Daily Values are based on a 2,000 calorie diet.

PARMESAN PEPPER MASHED POTATOES

Ingredients

- 4 potatoes, peeled and cubed
- 1 tbsp extra-virgin olive oil
- 1/2 C. diced red bell pepper
- 1/2 C. diced yellow bell pepper
- 1/4 C. all-purpose flour
- 2 C. chicken broth
- ground black pepper to taste
- 3 oz. baby spinach leaves
- 1/2 C. grated Parmesan cheese
- 2 tbsps bacon bits
- 1 tbsp minced garlic
- 2 tbsps butter
- 1/2 C. cream
- salt and pepper to taste

Directions

- Get your potatoes boiling in water and salt, set the heat to low, place a lid on the pot, and let everything cook for 22 mins.
- Remove all the liquids and let the potatoes cool a bit.
- Begin to stir fry your bell peppers in olive oil for 5 mins then add in the flour and continue cooking everything for 4 more mins.

- Now add the broth and get everything boiling.
- Let the mix cook for 17 mins then add some black pepper.
- Remove the liquid from the potatoes then combine the spuds with: the garlic, baby spinach, bacon bits, and parmesan.
- Begin to partially mash the potatoes then add in the cream and butter and mash the potatoes fully until smooth.
- When serving the potatoes top them liberally with the gravy.
- Enjoy.

Amount per serving (6 total)

Timing Information:

Preparation	20 m
Cooking	25 m
Total Time	45 m

Nutritional Information:

Calories	301 kcal
Fat	16.1 g
Carbohydrates	32.3g
Protein	8.2 g
Cholesterol	45 mg
Sodium	231 mg

* Percent Daily Values are based on a 2,000 calorie diet.

MASHED POTATOES BITES

Ingredients

- 1/2 C. vegetable oil for frying
- 1 1/2 C. milk
- 1 egg
- 1 (7.6 oz.) package garlic flavored instant mashed potatoes
- 2 tsps salt
- 2 tsps ground black pepper
- 1 1/2 lbs chicken tenders

Directions

- Get a bowl, combine: eggs and milk.
- At the same time begin to get your oil hot.
- Get a 2nd bowl and combine the potatoes with pepper and salt.
- Coat your pieces of chicken with the milk mix then dredge the chicken in the dry mix.
- Fry the chicken for 9 mins until browned on both sides.
- Enjoy.

Amount per serving (6 total)

Timing Information:

Preparation	10 m
Cooking	10 m
Total Time	20 m

Nutritional Information:

Calories	556 kcal
Fat	25.7 g
Carbohydrates	34.8g
Protein	44.5 g
Cholesterol	139 mg
Sodium	945 mg

* Percent Daily Values are based on a 2,000 calorie diet.

Sour Cream, Cheddar, and Mashed Potatoes

Ingredients

- 7 large potatoes, peeled and cubed
- 1 (10 oz.) package frozen chopped spinach, thawed and drained
- 1 C. sour cream
- 1/4 C. butter
- 2 tbsps chopped green onions
- 2 tsps salt
- 1/4 tsp black pepper
- 1 C. shredded Cheddar cheese

Directions

- Coat a baking dish with oil then set your oven to 400 degrees before doing anything else.
- Get your potatoes boiling in water and salt for 17 mins then remove the liquids and begin to partially mash the potatoes in a bowl.

- Add in: the pepper, spinach, salt, sour cream, green onions, and butter.
- Fully mash the potatoes until everything is smooth then spread the mix into the baking dish.
- Cook the spuds in the oven for 17 mins then lay your cheese over everything. Let the potatoes cook for 7 more mins.
- Enjoy.

Amount per serving (8 total)

Timing Information:

Preparation	20 m
Cooking	20 m
Total Time	40 m

Nutritional Information:

Calories	430 kcal
Fat	17 g
Carbohydrates	61.2g
Protein	10.8 g
Cholesterol	43 mg
Sodium	766 mg

* Percent Daily Values are based on a 2,000 calorie diet.

MASHED POTATOES NOODLES

Ingredients

- 1/4 C. chopped fresh green chile peppers
- 1 tbsp coarsely chopped garlic
- 2 tbsps fresh ginger, peeled and coarsely chopped
- 1 tsp salt
- 1/8 tsp ground turmeric
- 2 tsps vegetable oil
- 1 lb potatoes, peeled
- 3 C. water
- 3 1/2 C. chickpea flour
- 2 1/2 tsps salt
- 1 tsp ground turmeric
- 2 tbsps mustard oil
- vegetable oil for deep frying

Directions

- Place the following into the bowl of a food processor: 2 tbsps veggie oil, chilies, 1/8 tsp turmeric, garlic, 1 tsp salt, and ginger.
- Process the mix until it is smooth.
- Get your potatoes boiling in water and salt, set the heat to low, place a lid on the pot, and let everything cook for 17 mins.
- Place the potatoes in a bowl and begin to mash them.

- Try to get everything very smooth by adding in some of the water from boiling.
- Add in 1 tbsp of green chili paste, mustard oil, chickpea flour, 1 tsp turmeric, 2.5 tsps of salt.
- Then add in some more potato water and form a dough from the mix.
- Now get your oil hot in a deep pan and use a potato ricer to fry noodles for 3 mins.
- Fry all the potatoes in this manner.
- Enjoy.

Amount per serving (8 total)

Timing Information:

Preparation	45 m
Cooking	40 m
Total Time	1 h 25 m

Nutritional Information:

Calories	336 kcal
Fat	18.4 g
Carbohydrates	35.2g
Protein	9.4 g
Cholesterol	0 mg
Sodium	1024 mg

* Percent Daily Values are based on a 2,000 calorie diet.

EASTERN EUROPEAN STYLE MASHED POTATOES

Ingredients

- 1 large kohlrabi bulb, peeled and cut into cubes
- 6 small red potatoes
- 2 tsps grated garlic scape
- 1/2 C. shredded mozzarella cheese

Directions

- Set your oven to 325 degrees before doing anything else.
- Get your kohlrabi boiling in water and salt for 17 mins.
- At the same time place the potatoes in a bowl and cook them in the microwave for 12 mins.
- Get a bowl, combine: garlic, potatoes, and kohlrabi.
- Use a mixer to mash everything together until it is smooth.
- Then place everything into a baking dish and layer your cheese over the mix.
- Cook the contents in the oven for 35 mins.

- Let the dish sit for 10 mins before serving.
- Enjoy.

Amount per serving (6 total)

Timing Information:

Preparation	10 m
Cooking	55 m
Total Time	1 h 5 m

Nutritional Information:

Calories	154 kcal
Fat	1.8 g
Carbohydrates	29.8g
Protein	6.2 g
Cholesterol	6 mg
Sodium	76 mg

* Percent Daily Values are based on a 2,000 calorie diet.

MASCARPONE RUSSETS

Ingredients

- 4 1/2 lbs russet potatoes, peeled and halved lengthwise
- 1/2 C. mascarpone cheese at room temperature
- 1 egg yolk
- 3/4 C. milk
- salt and freshly ground black pepper to taste
- 1 pinch cayenne pepper, or to taste
- 1 C. butter, cut into chunks

Directions

- Get your potatoes boiling in water and salt, set the heat to low, and let everything cook for 17 mins.
- Remove the liquids then set your oven to 425 degrees before doing anything else.
- Get a bowl and begin to mix your mascarpone until it is soft then add in the milk and egg yolk.

- Continue to beat the mix until it is smooth again then add in the cayenne, black pepper, and salt.
- Mash the potatoes partially then add in the butter and mash the mix fully then add some pepper and salt.
- Add the cheese mix to the potatoes and mash everything again to evenly distribute the cheese.
- Lay your potatoes into a casserole dish and cook everything in the oven for 25 mins.
- Enjoy.

Amount per serving (8 total)

Timing Information:

Preparation	15 m
Cooking	35 m
Total Time	55 m

Nutritional Information:

Calories	483 kcal
Fat	30.7 g
Carbohydrates	47.3g
Protein	7.8 g
Cholesterol	106 mg
Sodium	243 mg

* Percent Daily Values are based on a 2,000 calorie diet.

FRENCH STYLE MASHED POTATOES

Ingredients

- 1 tsp butter, or as needed
- 5 potatoes, peeled and cut into large chunks
- 1 C. light cream
- 1 (8 oz.) package cream cheese, softened
- 1 egg
- 1 dash hot pepper sauce (such as Tabasco(R)), or to taste
- salt and ground black pepper to taste
- 1/4 C. chopped scallions

Directions

- Coat a casserole dish with butter then set your oven to 350 degrees before doing anything else.
- Get your potatoes boiling in water and salt, set the heat to low, and let the spuds cook for 22 mins.
- Now remove all the liquids and begin to partially mash the potatoes in a bowl.

- Add in the egg, cream cheese, and cream.
- Fully mash the mix.
- Layer everything into the casserole dish and cook the contents in the oven for 50 mins.
- Enjoy.

Amount per serving (6 total)

Timing Information:

Preparation	10 m
Cooking	1 h 5 m
Total Time	1 h 15 m

Nutritional Information:

Calories	364 kcal
Fat	22.4 g
Carbohydrates	33.8g
Protein	8.6 g
Cholesterol	100 mg
Sodium	155 mg

* Percent Daily Values are based on a 2,000 calorie diet.

Mashed Potatoes Appetizer

Ingredients

- 9 large potatoes
- 8 oz. cream cheese
- 1 C. sour cream
- 2 tsps onion salt
- 1 tbsp tarragon
- 1 tbsp parsley
- 1/4 jalapeno, seeds removed, diced
- 1 tsp salt
- 1/4 tsp ground black pepper
- 2 tbsps butter

Directions

- Coat a baking dish with oil then set your oven to 350 degrees before doing anything else.
- Get your potatoes boiling in water and salt for 15 mins or until you find the potatoes are soft.

- Place the potatoes in a bowl and being to partially mash them.
- Add in the pepper, cream cheese, salt, onion salt, sour cream, tarragon, parsley, and diced jalapenos.
- Mash everything until it is smooth then spread the mix into the baking dish and cook the contents in the oven for 33 mins.
- Enjoy.

Amount per serving (8 total)

Timing Information:

Preparation	10 m
Cooking	45 m
Total Time	55 m

Nutritional Information:

Calories	506 kcal
Fat	19.2 g
Carbohydrates	74.7g
Protein	11.5 g
Cholesterol	51 mg
Sodium	888 mg

* Percent Daily Values are based on a 2,000 calorie diet.

HOLIDAY SWEET MASHED POTATOES

Ingredients

- 6 oranges
- 3 C. cooked, mashed sweet potatoes
- 1 C. white sugar
- 1/4 C. orange juice
- 2 eggs, lightly beaten
- 1 tsp vanilla extract
- 1 C. butter, softened, divided
- 1 tbsp grated orange peel
- 1 C. brown sugar
- 1/2 tsp all-purpose flour
- 1 C. chopped pecans

Directions

- Set your oven to 350 degrees before doing anything else.
- Slice off the tops of your onions then remove the insides.
- Get a bowl, combine: grated orange, sweet potatoes, 1/2 C. butter, sugar, vanilla extract, orange juice, and eggs.
- Mash the mix until it is smooth then fill your oranges with it.
- Lay everything into the baking dish.
- Get the following heating in a pot: pecan, 1/2 C. butter, flour, and brown sugar.

- Heat and stir the mix until everything is even then top your oranges with the mix liberally.
- Add in enough water to fill the dish halfway and cook everything in the oven for 35 mins.
- Enjoy.

Amount per serving (6 total)

Timing Information:

Preparation	20 m
Cooking	30 m
Total Time	50 m

Nutritional Information:

Calories	854 kcal
Fat	45.9 g
Carbohydrates	110.1g
Protein	8 g
Cholesterol	143 mg
Sodium	293 mg

* Percent Daily Values are based on a 2,000 calorie diet.

Thanks for Reading! Join the Club and Keep on Cooking with 6 More Cookbooks....

http://bit.ly/1TdrStv

 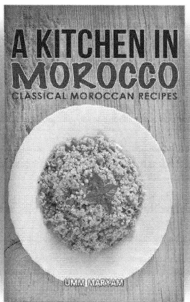 

To grab the box sets simply follow the link mentioned above, or tap one of book covers.

This will take you to a page where you can simply enter your email address and a PDF version of the box sets will be emailed to you.

Hope you are ready for some serious cooking!

http://bit.ly/1TdrStv

Come On...
Let's Be Friends :)

We adore our readers and love connecting with them socially.

Like BookSumo on Facebook and let's get social!

Facebook

And also check out the BookSumo Cooking Blog.

Food Lover Blog